A day in the life of
Pradeep the dentist

Monica Hughes

Heinemann
LIBRARY

Little Nippers

www.heinemann.co.uk/library
Visit our website to find out more information about **Heinemann Library** books.

To order:
☎ Phone 44 (0) 1865 888066
▤ Send a fax to 44 (0) 1865 314091
💻 Visit the Heinemann Bookshop at www.heinemann.co.uk/library to browse our catalogue and order online.

First published in Great Britain by Heinemann Library, Halley Court, Jordan Hill, Oxford OX2 8EJ, part of Harcourt Education.
Heinemann is a registered trademark of Harcourt Education Ltd.

Editorial: Jilly Attwood and Claire Throp
Design: Jo Hinton-Malivoire and bigtop, Bicester, UK
Models made by: Jo Brooker
Picture Research: Catherine Bevan
Production: Lorraine Warner

Originated by Dot Gradations
Printed and bound in China by South China Printing Company

ISBN 0 431 16522 X (hardback)
06 05 04 03 02
10 9 8 7 6 5 4 3 2 1

ISBN 0 431 16527 0 (paperback)
06 05 04 03 02
10 9 8 7 6 5 4 3 2 1

British Library Cataloguing in Publication Data
Hughes, Monica
    A day in the life of a dentist
    617.6′0232
A full catalogue record for this book is available from the British Library.

Acknowledgements
The publishers would like to thank the following for permission to reproduce photographs:
All photos by Trevor Clifford.

Cover photograph reproduced with permission of Trevor Clifford.

Special thanks to Dr Pradeep and his family.

The publishers would like to thank Annie Davy for her assistance in the preparation of this book.

Every effort has been made to contact copyright holders of any material reproduced in this book. Any omissions will be rectified in subsequent printings if notice is given to the publishers.

Contents

Meet Pradeep the dentist

This is Pradeep
the dentist.

This is the surgery where he works.

DENTAL SURGERY
tel. B/Stortford
507695
(24 HR.)
PREVENTION IS OUR PRACTICE

Have you ever been to
see a dentist?

Ready for work

Pradeep gets up early and has breakfast with his family.

He takes his children to school before he goes to work.

The day starts

Pradeep finds out
which patients have
come to see him.

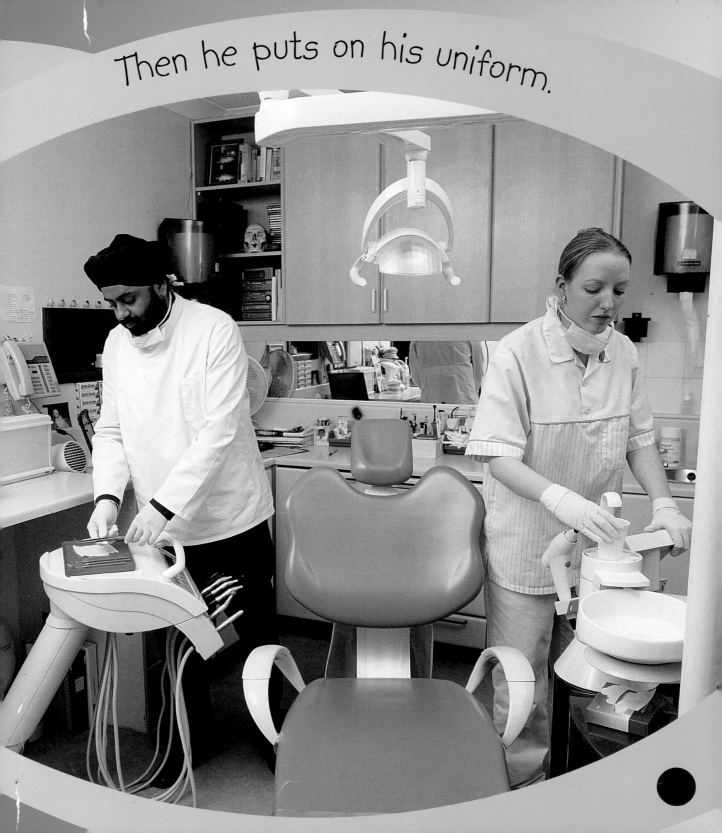

Then he puts on his uniform.

The first patient

Warren has come
to the dentist for
a check-up.

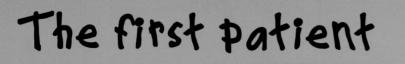

Pradeep shows Warren
his special chair.

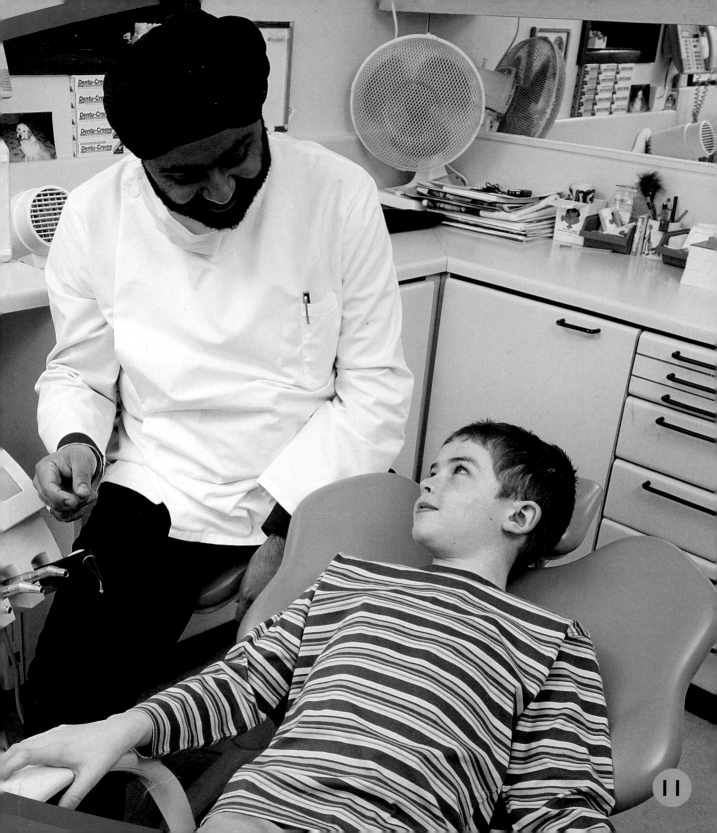

The check-up

Pradeep looks inside Warren's mouth.

Everything is fine.
Warren gets a sticker.

More patients

Pradeep gives the next
patient an injection.

Another patient has an
X-ray taken of her teeth.

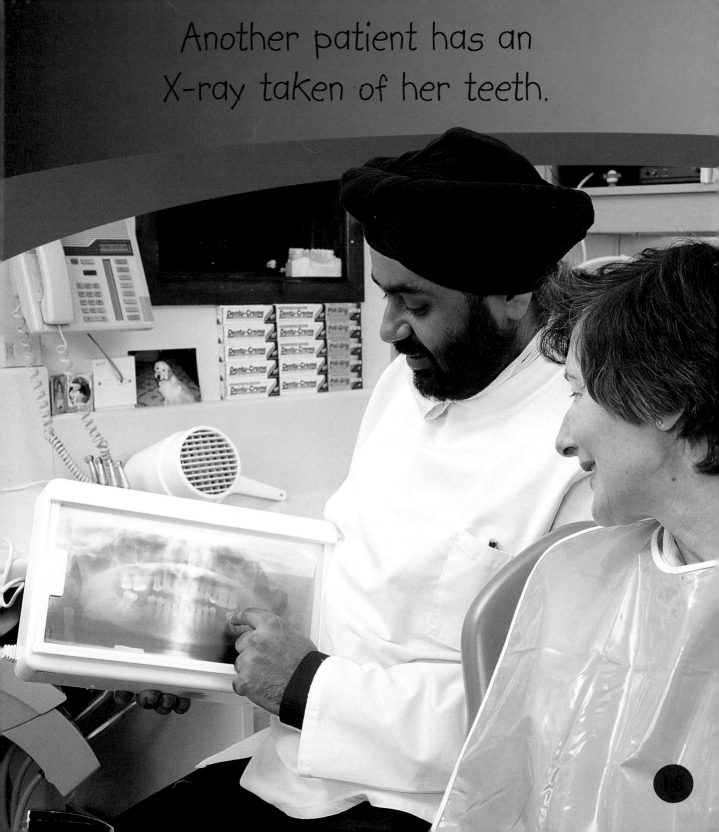

A break for lunch

After he sees lots more patients Pradeep is ready for his lunch.

After lunch he works on his computer.

A school visit

In the afternoon
Pradeep visits
a school.

19

Looking after teeth

Pradeep talks to the children about looking after their teeth.

He checks that Simon
can clean his teeth properly.

Pradeep remembers to clean his teeth before he goes to bed.

Index

The end

Notes for adults

This series supports the young child's exploration of their learning environment and their knowledge and understanding of their world. The following Early Learning Goals are relevant to the series:
• Respond to significant experiences, showing a range of feelings when appropriate.
• Find out about events that they observe.
• Ask questions about why things happen and how things work.
• Find out about and identify the uses of everyday technology to support their learning.

The series shows the different jobs four professionals do and provides opportunities to compare and contrast them. The books show that like everyone else, including young children, they get up in the morning, go to bed at night, break for meals, and have families, pets and a life outside their work.

The books will help the child to extend their vocabulary, as they will hear new words. Some of the words that may be new to them in **A Day in the Life of a Dentist** are *surgery*, *patients*, '*check-up*', *injection* and *X-ray*. Since words are used in context in the book this should enable the young child to gradually incorporate them into their own vocabulary.

The following additional information may be of interest:
The dentist wears a mask and thin latex gloves when examining a patient, as does the dental nurse. The patients also wear bibs to protect their clothes. The dentist demonstrates the correct way for children to brush their teeth – up and down rather than side to side – using a squeeze of toothpaste the size of a pea.

Follow-up activities
The child could role play situations in a dental surgery. Areas could be set up to create a consulting room, a waiting room and a reception area. The child could also record what they have found out by drawing, painting or tape recording their experiences.